Albert Einstein

The incredible life, discoveries, stories and lessons of Einstein!

Table of Contents

Introduction

Thank you for taking the time to pick up this book: *"Albert Einstein: The incredible life, discoveries, stories and lessons of Einstein!"*.

This book talks about the life story of Albert Einstein and shares some of his greatest moments. As you go though Einstein's milestones, you will pick up valuable life lessons that will make your own journey a more fulfilled one as well.

You will discover stories of Einstein's childhood, career path, and his most notable discoveries and moments. Studying the journey of such an incredible man will provide you with a depth of knowledge on how to duplicate his success in your chosen field.

At the completion of this book, you will have a good understanding of Einstein's incredible journey and will be able to use his experiences to enhance your own life!

Once again, thanks for reading this book, I hope you enjoy it and find it helpful!

Chapter 1:
The Early Years

To say that Albert Einstein was a great man is an understatement because he was not just great. He was brilliant, phenomenal, and exceptional. Albert Einstein simply was incomparable. Even today, in this modern day and age where inventors and other brilliant minds abound, Einstein still remains known as the world's quintessential genius.

This genius, like almost all geniuses during their own time, was not always recognized for his exceptional mind. In fact, during his early years in school, one of his teachers had said that he would not amount to much – a statement which Einstein would later prove to be untrue.

Einstein's Background and Early Life

Albert Einstein was born in Germany's city of Ulm on March 14, 1879. His father was an engineer and salesman named Hermann Einstein and his mother was a talented musician whose maiden name was Pauline Koch. His parents were of Jewish descent but it is not known if they were devout practicing Jews. He had one sibling named Maria who everyone referred to as Maja. She was born 2 years after Albert.

When Einstein was one, his father moved the entire family to Munich. Einstein's father and his uncle Jakob wanted to start an electrical engineering company together. They named the company Einstein & Cie. Einstein spent most of his childhood in Munich because of this move. A year after they moved to Munich, on November 18, 1881, Maja was born.

Einstein had a fairly normal childhood. He was a healthy boy with a curious and inquisitive disposition. His sister describes in her book that she wrote in 1924 that her older brother was a calm and dreamy child. The only thing that bothered his parents about him when he was young was the fact that he did not learn to speak until much later than the other children. Einstein himself confirmed this when he told his biographer as much. He said that his parents worried so much that there was something wrong with him because he was unable to talk at the time when he was expected to have already learned how. They even consulted a doctor to ask if there was a medical reason as to why he wasn't speaking.

Einstein's relatives and teachers mistook his inability to verbally express himself as a sign of someone who was dull and slow. It was even observed that before the age of seven, Einstein would repeat his sentences softly to himself which strengthened other people's belief that he was indeed dimwitted. Modern theorists hypothesize that maybe Einstein had a slight autism or was dyslexic, and that that's why he was unable to speak early on. Still, this did not stop Einstein from becoming a great scientist.

While Einstein was growing up, he showed great interest in the sciences. At the tender age of five, Einstein had his first encounter with the wonders of science when his father gave him a compass. The compass captivated the young Albert Einstein. He was so fascinated by the fact that no matter which way he turned, the needle of the compass always pointed north. He also learned how to play the violin and the piano at a very young age. Still, the people around him did not think that he would be the genius that people today know him to be.

To make sure that Albert was ready for school, his parents had him tutored privately for one year. After that he was sent to a

Catholic primary school. During his stay at the Catholic school where his parents had enrolled him, Einstein's teachers did not think of him as exceptional or talented. Most of them thought that Einstein was just a regular student. But given that he later on got accepted to one of the hardest schools to get into, that might not have been true at all. At age 9, he was accepted to the Luitpold-Gymnasium which was considered to be a school where some of the best and brightest attended. He would not have been able to get in that school if he was just an average student with average grades.

During his time in school, Einstein was known to have challenged the rigidity of the rote learning methods of the schools that he had attended. Rote learning in a general sense focuses on memorization and repetition in order to remember the concepts and ideas but not always understanding what is being memorized. He felt that this form of teaching style curbs creativity and lets original thought take a backseat. He also felt that the same strict teaching methods didn't really allow students to learn much. Because of this, Einstein had a lot of altercations with his instructors and even the higher authorities of the schools that he attended.

As Einstein was growing up, he got more exposed to the sciences from an informal tutor named Max Talmud (Talmey). Max was a Polish student studying medicine who often joined the Einstein family for meals. He fed young Albert's mind and curiosity by introducing him to various texts about mathematics, science and philosophy. This inspired the upcoming young scientist to start thinking about how things work and further fueled his curious mind. Because of this curiosity, he was able to later on formulate and write what is considered to be his first major paper. He started writing his first major paper entitled "The Investigation of the State of

Ether (Aether) in Magnetic Fields " in 1894 when he was just in his teens.

Over the years, his father's engineering business started to fail. Einstein's father again decided to move the family to Milan in Italy around mid-1890s in search for greener pastures. Einstein was told to remain in Munich to continue his studies.

Einstein left the Luitpold Gymnasium soon after. There were many theories as to why he left. One was that he was asked to leave by the school's administration because they could no longer tolerate his behavior towards the teaching staff and how opposed he was to the learning style of the school. The other and the most plausible was the probability that he just didn't want to remain in a school that promoted rote learning.

Einstein in the University

Albert joined his family in Milan after he left school. He later on applied to the Swiss Federal Polytechnic School in Zurich. On his first attempt to take the admissions test, he failed in some of the portions of the exam like the languages portion. It was said that Albert was not very good with languages and that for the longest time the only language he was comfortable with was German. Though he failed to pass the entire exam, it was noted that his grades in the mathematics and physics portions were very high.

Einstein was still very young when he took the exam at the Swiss Federal Polytechnic School. Because of this, he was advised to finish his pre-university education at Aarau in Switzerland. In Aarau, Einstein stayed with the schoolmaster Joel Winteler. Joel had a daughter named Marie with whom Einstein had fallen in love. During his stay in Aarau, he received notice that he was to report for military service back in Germany. He didn't want to go through with the military service so, with the approval from his parents, he renounced his German citizenship. He later on became a Swiss citizen.

On his second attempt, he passed the exam with good grades overall and was soon enrolled in the 4-year mathematics and physics teaching diploma. He was 17 when he started the 4-year teaching course. During his stay at the university, he met his future wife Mileva Maric. He finished his degree in 1900. One year after he graduated he received his Swiss citizenship.

Chapter 2:
Life after the University

You'd think that a genius like Einstein would have gotten a job in the field of academics or something similar right away. But as it happened, it was not yet meant to be. He really did try to get a teaching position at various universities but was met with regrets. This was mainly due to not so flattering recommendations from his former professors in college. Einstein's reputation as someone who constantly challenged authorities made it hard for him to find employment.

About 2 years after he graduated and with the help of the father of one of his former classmates, Einstein found a job in the Federal Office for Intellectual Property, otherwise known as the Patent office. At the Federal Office for Intellectual Property, Einstein was employed as an assistant examiner. The job was considered to be menial and Einstein was able to complete his tasks within a few hours. The rest of his time at the office was spent formulating, reading, and writing papers about his theories. He busied himself with various scientific researches and was never idle.

In 1903, he became a permanent employee of the Federal Office for Intellectual Property and moved on to evaluating patents that involved electromagnetic devices. It was also in the year 1903 that he married his first wife Mileva Maric.

Einstein's job was so easy for him that he was able to complete his tasks well before the working hours of the day had finished. He had so much free time at the Federal Office for Intellectual Property that he was able to write 4 of the most important papers in the history of scientific discoveries. These papers were as follows: the photoelectric effect, the Brownian motion, the special theory of relativity and the mass and energy equivalence. In 1905, he was able to publish all 4 papers in the Annalen der Physik, one of the most notable physics journal of that time. The year 1905 was considered to be Einstein's miracle year or the Annus Mirabilis.

The four papers that Einstein published were at first met with silence from the scientific community. No one specializing in the field of physics took notice of the papers that an ordinary patent office employee had written. He was not considered as scientist yet so nobody paid attention to his works. It depressed Einstein that his most important discoveries seemed irrelevant. It wasn't until Einstein's theories were backed by Max Planck that his papers got the distinction that they deserved. Planck who was already a famed quantum theorist at that time understood how ground-breaking Einstein's discoveries were and backed him up with his own take on the subject matter.

Within the same year of his papers being published, Einstein obtained his doctors degree. He was also thrust into the limelight soon after as more and more scientists marveled at his discoveries. He became almost instantly famous all over the world. He was invited to speaking engagements at some of the most prestigious universities to talk about his papers. He was also offered various teaching posts in various universities in Europe.

In 1908, Einstein was appointed Privatdozant in Bern. The term Privatdozent refers to a university lecturer who isn't on the payroll of the university but may teach the students in the subject that he specializes in. The lecturer's fees came directly from his students and not from the university. Even in this modern day and age, this academic title is common in German speaking countries though the salary arrangement might be slightly different.

The following year, Einstein became Professor Extraordinary in Zurich. Soon after, in 1911, he quit his job at the Federal Office for Intellectual Property and his position in Zurich to become a full-pledged professor of Theoretical Physics at the Karl-Ferdinand University of Prague. At that point, Einstein was clearly on his way to the top of his academic aspirations.

In 1914, he returned to Germany to take on the position of Director of the Kaiser Wilhelm Physical Institute. He was also a professor in the Humboldt University of Berlin at that time. It was said that he had a special clause in his contract with the Humboldt University of Berlin that freed him from a lot of the teaching obligations that come with being a professor. In the same year, Einstein got his German citizenship back. He stayed in Berlin and went on as director until 1933.

1916 was another great year for Einstein as this was the year when he was appointed as the president of the German Physical Society. He held on to this prestigious position for two years. While he was enjoying his appointment as president, he also attained membership of the Prussian Academy of Sciences.

Everything eventually turned around for Einstein after his papers were published. Where he once had trouble finding a job, his offers came in left and right soon after his papers got published.

Einstein stayed in Germany until 1933. Then he once again renounced his German citizenship for political reasons. It was also during this time that the German dictator Adolf Hitler had risen to power. Theorists believe that Einstein's move to renounce his citizenship once again was a form of defiant act to the Hitler dictatorship. Einstein was a pacifist so he chose to leave the country and move to the United States.

When he and his wife emigrated to the United States, Einstein became a professor of Theoretical Physics in Princeton, New Jersey. He enjoyed a fairly regular life in America with his wife. During his time in America, Einstein received word that the Nazis were trying to build a weapon of mass destruction. This weapon was the atomic bomb. Einstein was so horrified at the idea that the Nazis would have a weapon that could destroy so many lives that on August 2, 1939 he wrote a letter to President Franklin D. Roosevelt to alert him of what he had discovered. In his letter, he detailed the dangers of having this type of weapon in the hands of the Nazis. He urged the president to find a way to counter act or neutralize the weapon before the Nazis could complete it. He also told the president to intensify the country's research on nuclear weapons.

After reading Einstein's letter, the president acted not only by increasing research on nuclear powered weapons, but also by requesting that the United States create their own atomic bomb before the Nazis complete theirs. The race to build the first atomic bomb was on and the winner was the United States. Though the letter was the only contribution that Einstein made towards the creation of the atomic bomb, his name later on became closely associated with the weapon. Some even call him the father of the atomic bomb because of 2 important reasons. The first reason was that it was his letter that became the catalyst that urged the United States to create the first one, and the second is that his famous equation $E=mc^2$ made creating the bomb possible.

Einstein acquired a US citizenship in 1940. He also kept his Swiss citizenship. In 1945, he retired from his post in

Princeton. By this time, Einstein had already accomplished so much and had become widely recognized everywhere he went. People would call out to him as if he was some sort of celebrity and he was invited to a lot of important events. He became an honorary member of various organizations relating to the sciences even without asking to be inducted into the groups. He was even once asked to be the president of the State of Israel but he politely declined the offer.

On April 15, 1955 Einstein was taken to the hospital because he had a ruptured abdominal aortic aneurysm. Doctors wanted to take him into surgery to fix the problem but Einstein insisted that he did not want to prolong his life using artificial methods. He died 3 days later on April 18 at the age of 76. His body was cremated soon after, but where his ashes were scattered remains a mystery to this day.

Chapter 3:
Einstein's Most Notable Works and Awards

It is undeniable that Einstein has contributed a lot to science. His lifelong passion for discovering how the world works made him one of the most important persons in history. Time magazine even called him the Person of the Century in 1999. He was chosen for his many contributions to science and to the world in general.

While the title Person of the Century sounds very grand, nothing compares to the title of Nobel Prize winner. In 1922, Einstein won the Nobel Prize in Physics for the year 1921 for his various contributions and services to Theoretical Physics. This very prestigious award that only a handful of the world population receives was given to Einstein for his work on photoelectric effect.

Other achievements and awards that Einstein attained include:

1. In 1925, Einstein was given the Copley Medal by the Royal Society of London. This award is the oldest and most prestigious award given by the distinguished society. The annual award recognizes those with outstanding achievements in scientific research. This award was first given in 1731, long before the Nobel Prize started handing out their awards.

2. Einstein was the first recipient of the Max Planck medal for the German Physical Society. He was awarded this medal in 1929 in Berlin, Germany.

3. Albert Einstein was awarded the Gold Medal of the Royal Astronomical Society in 1926.

4. Einstein received the Franklin Institute's Franklin Medal in 1936, also for his work on photoelectric effect and his extensive work on relativity.

5. The International Union of Pure and Applied Science declared 2005 as the World Year of Physics in celebration of the 100th year anniversary of Einstein's 4 most important published papers.

6. Though technically not an award, Einstein's name was forever immortalized in the periodic table after one of the elements was named after him in 1955. The chemical element 99 was called einsteinium. It was named after him four months after his death.

7. A medical school in New York City was named after Einstein. It is called The Albert Einstein College of Medicine.

8. On a hill in Telegrafenberg in Potsdam, Germany, stands the Albert Einstein Science Park. Within the grounds of the park is the famous Einstein Tower which is an astrophysical observatory. When you enter the building, you will see a bronze bust of Albert Einstein.

9. Einstein also received various honorary doctorates from some of the best universities all over the world. He held honorary doctorates from Princeton University, University of Madrid, ETH in Zurich, Oxford University and Harvard University to name a few.

10. Einstein's name was added to the Walhalla Temple in Donaustauf, Bavaria in 1990 where other names of "laudable and distinguished Germans" are placed.

11. The Albert Einstein Memorial resides in Washington DC. The bronze statue depicts Einstein as seated while he is holding a manuscript in his hand.

12. The US Postal Service honored Einstein by including him in the Prominent Americans Series which ran from 1965 to 1978. The stamp was issued in 1966 and was worth 8 cents.

13. Albert Einstein was inducted into the New Jersey Hall of Fame in 2008.

Einstein achieved world fame through his contributions to science. His works revolutionized the world of physics and its effect can still be felt today. The principles of some of the modern technologies today are still based on a lot of Einstein's discoveries.

Albert Einstein's Most Notable Works

Before he became the multi-awarded scientist that he is, Einstein was already brilliant and was very talented not just in science but in the arts as well. His best and most notable works are listed below for reference.

1. The Annus Mirabilis Papers – The Annus Mirabilis papers were composed of 4 of Einstein's most notable works. They are as follows:

   a. The Photoelectric Effect – The first paper out of the 4 papers that Einstein published in 1905 was the paper on photoelectric effect. This was also the one that helped him win the 1921 Nobel Prize for Physics. It was published in June of 1905. The photoelectric effect states that light behaves as a wave and a particle.

b. The Brownian Motion – Einstein's second paper published in July of 1905 proved the existence of molecules. It also explained how molecules move and how big molecules really are.

c. The Theory of Special Relativity – The third paper published by Einstein in 1905 was released in September. This theory states that the speed of light is fixed or constant regardless of its source. It also states that time passes at different rates for objects moving at different speeds. This theory gave people the idea that time travel might be possible.

d. Mass and Energy Equivalence – The fourth paper of the Annus Mirabilis was published in November of 1905. This paper gave the world one of the most famous equations: $E = mc^2$ where E stands for energy, m stands for mass and c stands for the speed of light in a vacuum. This same formula became the basis for nuclear energy.

2. General Theory of Relativity – Einstein published the general theory of relativity in 1916 that soon became an essential tool in the understanding of things like gravitational lensing and black holes. This was his attempt at reconciling the laws of electromagnetic fields with the laws of mechanics.

3. Thermodynamic fluctuations and statistical physics – He attempted to explain the phenomenon that is the atom using statistics. These papers were closely tied to the Brownian motion papers.

4. Quantum theory of light – In his quantum theory of light, Einstein proposed that light is made up of separate packets of energy. He called them photons or quanta.

5. Einstein refrigerator – Einstein even dabbled in some smaller projects like this one. He created a refrigerator design that got a US patent in 1930. This design does not use Freon as a cooling agent. It runs on practically no energy. It uses butane, water, and ammonia. Scientists are currently taking another look at this invention as an environmentally-friendly alternative to current refrigeration and air-conditioning appliances.

These are just some of Einstein's major and most notable accomplishments and awards. There are also other minor papers and discoveries that he made that contributed a lot to science. He was forever trying to resolve the problems that physics presented in his own way. He liked to think out of the box and was constantly trying to find answers and explanations for how things around him worked. Even after he retired from his teaching post at the university he still tirelessly conducted experiments and had debates with fellow scientists about the various concepts relating to physics. His entire lifetime was devoted to science.

Chapter 4:
What Einstein Did in His Free Time

The greatest physicist of all time was not always devoted to the discovery of the photoelectric effect and special theories of relativity. He was, after all, only human just like anybody else. As he racked up award after award, he also had his own personal life to manage. He of course needed to socialize, to travel and enjoy himself just like any regular human being. But unlike regular people, Einstein was not at all ordinary.

Causes that Einstein Supported

When Einstein was younger, he was known as someone who always defied the authorities of the institutions that he had attended. Despite all this, he was not considered a problem child or a troublesome teen. His only reason for disagreeing with the authorities was due to his aversion to the teaching styles of the school. When he became a professor in the university he dispensed of rote learning altogether and taught his students using his own methods.

Many people know Einstein to be a pacifist. In the earlier chapter, it was noted that he renounced his citizenship the second time to get away from the Nazi regime. He was a Jew by birth and so he condemned the violent acts done by the Nazis to the Jews when Hitler was in power. Prior to his defection, the Nazi scientists were also attacking his theories saying that they were "Jewish Physics". Any professor known to be teaching Einstein's concepts were told to use the alternative "Aryan Physics" and were blacklisted if they did not comply. These forms of "harassment" prompted Einstein to leave Germany and move to the United States permanently.

His renunciation of his German citizenship was his pacifist way of fighting the Nazis.

The story of the atomic bomb also further cemented Einstein's position on violence and mass destruction. But for all his good intentions, Einstein unintentionally set in motion the start of the nuclear arms race when he wrote that letter to US president Franklin D. Roosevelt in 1939. His letter prompted the United States to create the country's own atomic bomb though that was not the action that Einstein was looking for. He was saddened when he learned that the US government, whom he turned to for help in stopping the Nazis from deploying a weapon of mass destruction, was responsible for the bombing of Hiroshima where thousands of lives were lost.

After all that had happened during World War II and the events surrounding the bombing of Japan, Einstein found a use for his unwanted fame by campaigning for nuclear disarmament. He also promoted internationalism and human rights. He was a famed advocate of international cooperation and had worked with the United Nations in unifying the different countries. He was a man who had been through two World Wars so it's no wonder that he would champion these types of causes.

Einstein was also very much into fighting for civil rights and anti-racism causes. He was said to have joined the National Association for the Advancement of Colored People (NAACP) while he was in Princeton to campaign for the rights of African Americans. He frequently corresponded with NAACP founder W. E. B. Du Bois and even offered to appear as character witness during his trial. When the judge learned that Einstein would want to appear for Du Bois, he was convinced to drop the case in order to avoid too much publicity. In one of his rare speeches Einstein condemned racism and called it "a disease of white people".

Einstein's Characteristics and Traits

Very little was written as to whether Einstein did things that ordinary boys did. There is no record of him getting into fist fights with other boys or if Einstein played any particular sport. He did not have any widely known vices nor did he engage in other activities that are deemed illegal. It's easy to conclude that Einstein was probably always buried in books and research and didn't have time to do such trivial things.

Outside of physics, Einstein showed promise in the field of music as well. This was probably due to the influence of his musician mother. He learned to play the violin at a very young age. He liked playing the instrument in front of an audience and he often performed whenever he felt stuck on something that he was working on. Soon after he finished playing, he would find a way to somehow resolve the problem.

Another thing that people remember fondly about Einstein was his quirky personality and even quirkier sense of humor. He was said to have enjoyed teasing his wife very much. While he was entertaining a group of intellectuals one time, he teased Mileva by telling his guests a risqué story while his wife was in their company. He was given a very sharp "Albert!" as a reprimand but was soon followed by a flirtatious giggle. Einstein treasures gag gifts from friends and would promptly display them in his home as if they were prized paintings.

Einstein never really felt comfortable with his fame. He was a very humble man who didn't really want to be thrust into the limelight but was forced into it after his contributions for science became widely known. He achieved celebrity status and was constantly followed by people - especially the paparazzi. He was asked to make speeches and give talks about his work but he often declined. His humility manifested in his appearance and actions. He dressed very casually and only made a fuss with his appearance when needed. He would tirelessly answer letters from people who admired his work and would promptly lend a hand to someone who was in need.

Chapter 5:
The Love and Family Life
of Albert Einstein

All work and no play make a man dull and boring. It is no wonder then that Einstein during his lifetime has had his fair share of falling in love.

Einstein's first known love was Marie Winteler who was the daughter of the schoolmaster Joel Winteler. He had stayed with the Wintelers during his teens and had fallen in love with the young Marie. In his letters that were recently published by the Hebrew University in Jerusalem, he disclosed how even as he was married to Mileva he still thought of Marie Winteler and had strong feelings about her still. He also spoke of a "missed life" with Winteler. There are currently no records that show if Einstein and Winteler did indeed get together romantically or intimately.

Mileva Maric was Einstein's first wife. She was of Serbian descent and was a fellow student at the university where Einstein was enrolled. Mileva was the only woman at that time taking up studies in the mathematical section of the university. Einstein and Maric married in January 6, 1903. Their union was witnessed by Maurice Solovine and Conrad Habicht. It was said that prior to their marriage in 1903 Einstein and Maric had a daughter named Lieserl born in 1902. The fate of their daughter was never discovered, for Maric returned to Zurich one day without the girl. It was said that she either succumbed to an illness or was set up for adoption while she was an infant. Until now, the real name and the whereabouts of Einstein's illegitimate daughter are unknown.

Throughout their marriage, Einstein considered Maric as his equal. He admired her intellect and her independence. He valued her opinions and often talked with her about the things that he was working on. His discussions with Maric often circled around topics related to science as they shared a common interest in physics.

Sadly, Einstein and Maric's marriage was not meant to be. In 1919, they divorced after living apart for 5 years. The primary reason for their divorce was Einstein's affair with his cousin Elsa Lowenthal since 1912. It was also found out through his recently published letters to Maric that Einstein had misogynistic tendencies. In his letters, Einstein outlined a set of rules for Maric to follow including a ban on intimate relations and living with a strict domestic arrangement. These were written at the time when Eistein requested for a divorce but Maric wanted to remain married. These rules obviously did not sit well with Maric and they divorced in 1919.

Einstein had two more children with Maric named Hans Albert and Eduard. Hans was born in 1904 in Bern while Eduard who arrived 6 years later in July 1910 was born in Zurich.

Hans Albert grew up to become a professor like his father but his specialty was in engineering. He married a woman named Frieda Knecht with whom he had 4 children. He lived a full life despite his parent's divorce. At the age of 69 he died due to heart failure.

His younger brother Eduard was not as fortunate. Eduard was so deeply affected by his parent's divorce in 1919 that he had a breakdown in 1920. He was also diagnosed with schizophrenia in the same year. Soon after his breakdown, Maric started caring for Eduard. She endured having to commit her son to various asylums until her death. When she died, Eduard was committed to an asylum permanently. Inside the asylum, Eduard had a stroke and died in 1965 at the age of 55.

Einstein and Lowenthal got married the same year that his divorce with Maric was finalized. At that time, Lowenthal already had 2 children from her previous marriage named Ilse and Margot. During his second take at married life, Einstein seemed more in love and acted more romantically towards his second wife. Unlike his letters to his first wife, Einstein's love letters to his second wife were peppered with words that expressed his desire to get intimate with her. He also signed his correspondence with "kisses from your Albert". Einstein's marriage to Lowenthal, though better than his marriage with Maric, was not ideal either. After 4 years of marriage it was said that Einstein again had another affair - this time with his secretary Bette Neuman. In December of 1936, Lowenthal died and Einstein's sister moved in with him.

Chapter 6:
Ten Interesting Facts about Albert Einstein's Life

Ever since his miracle year, Einstein's life became a matter of public interest. Like most celebrities who instantly rise to fame, people became curious of Einstein's personal life and sought to uncover his secrets. Here are 10 of the most interesting things about Einstein's life that have been uncovered so far.

1. He was on the FBI watch list – When Einstein and his wife moved to America, the government put him on the FBI watch list. The US government was afraid that Einstein might be a spy and would eventually sell his ideas of creating nuclear weapons to the enemies of the state. His left-wing causes also drew suspicions from the US government so they watched him closely for decades.

   The FBI was known to have rifled through Einstein's trash looking for evidence of his subversion and affiliation to the Soviets. FBI agents also listened in on his phone conversations and had also opened his mail to ensure that he was not doing any covert spying operations for the enemy. Nothing was ever proven and the decades-long surveillance project came up empty. By the time Einstein died in 1955 the FBI's file on him had over 1800 pages.

2. His brain was stolen – Einstein's final request before he died was that his body was to be cremated and scattered in an undisclosed location. This request was granted but not before his brain was stolen. Thomas Harvey, a

pathologist at Princeton removed Einstein's brain during his autopsy without that knowledge and consent of his family. He argued that he wanted to keep it and hoped that some future technology would be able to unlock the secrets of Einstein's genius mind.

Einstein's son reluctantly agreed to have his late father's brain be cut into pieces for various scientists all over the world to study. Since the 1980s there have been some studies done on Einstein's brain but no conclusive findings ever came into fruition. Most of the findings were either discredited or dismissed. The most notable among all the findings was probably the paper published by a Canadian university in 1999. In the paper, they claimed that Einstein's parietal lobe, a part of the brain that was commonly associated with spatial and mathematical abilities, had an unusual set of folds. Notable as it was, this claim was not proven.

3. Einstein's Nobel Prize winnings became part of his divorce settlement – 1916 was the year when Einstein first asked Maric for a divorce. His wife became distraught and withdrew herself for about a year. She was so distressed that she was said to have become bedridden for a time and was unable to care for her children. Maric's sister had to come in to help take care of the children while she was indisposed.

When she had come to and agreed to a divorce with Einstein, she stipulated that any winnings Einstein might have earned should he win the Nobel Prize would be given to her. In 1921 Einstein won and he gave all his winnings to Maric together with an annual stipend.

4. He owned a comb but he kept forgetting to use it –
    Many people have repeatedly asked why Einstein's hair
    in most of his photos looked unkempt and unruly.

    The reason for his wild hairstyle started when his first
    son Hans Albert was born. His son would wake up
    crying in the wee hours of the morning usually
    requiring a change of underpants and some milk. The
    constant sleep interruption made Einstein forgetful of
    things that he considered as non-essential like
    grooming or names of people he met etc. This is why he
    often forgot to comb his hair among other things.

    After his death, his unintentional signature hairstyle
    would become an iconic part of history and pop culture.
    People would instantly recognize Einstein based on his
    hair alone. People would forever associate the wild hair
    with a genius.

5. The photo of Einstein sticking his tongue out was real –
    That iconic photo was not photo-shopped and was
    indeed real. It was taken by Arthur Sasse on Einstein's
    72nd birthday. As the story goes, he and his friends had
    been celebrating his birthday at the Princeton Club with
    so much merriment. As he was about to go home, press
    photographers were waiting for him outside the club
    and had requested that he smile for the cameras. He
    was already tired from an entire night of partying so
    instead of a smile he stuck his tongue out in an attempt
    to ruin the photograph. His efforts backfired and the
    photograph became one of the most iconic
    photographs. It has been used by various pop culture
    artists to inject some humor into Einstein's genius.
    Einstein himself liked the photo so much that he asked

the photographer to send him copies which he later on used as for his Christmas cards.

6. Einstein had a huge head and was fat – When Einstein was born, his relatives had described him as a fat baby with a large head. His mother thought that his head was so big that she thought that Einstein might have been deformed somehow. His family even considered his large head a monstrosity. A physician dispelled these notions saying that Einstein's head still fell under the range of normal sized heads and eventually pacified his family. Little did they know that his large head contained the brains that would help him win the Nobel Prize for Physics.

7. Einstein was a lady's man – It was no secret that Einstein cheated on his first wife with his cousin Elsa Lowenthal. He later married Lowenthal but not before considering marrying her eldest daughter Ilse first. Ilse did not find Einstein attractive and only saw him as a father figure so the union never happened.

    During his marriage to Lowenthal, Einstein had a string of affairs including one with his secretary Bette Neuman. In the recent Einstein letters published by the Hebrew University in Jerusalem it was found that he had spent time with 6 other women with whom he had also received gifts and favors from. All this happened while he was married to Lowenthal. The identities of the women mentioned in the journals remain unknown as they were only identified by their first names and sometimes only by their initials.

8. Einstein loved sailing – On his 50th birthday, someone gave Einstein a boat. He loved sailing but he was never

good at it. He was rescued often after failing to properly manage the boat.

9. Einstein was very well travelled – After his papers came out, Einstein got invited to speaking engagements, debates and various studies and grants all over the world. He had travelled to Japan, Singapore and Ceylon in 1922 on a 6-month excursion and speaking tour. He even met the Emperor and Empress at Japan's Imperial Palace. His travel to Asia made him unable to personally accept his Nobel Prize for Physics award. Einstein also traveled to Palestine where he was met by the head of the state and was given a cannon salute upon his arrival.

    Other places he had travelled to included London and Switzerland. In the United States he had been to New York, Washington DC, Columbia and California.

10. He was friends with Charlie Chaplin – Carl Laemmle once took Einstein on a tour of Universal Studios where he was the head. It is during this tour that he met Charlie Chaplin. The two instantly hit it off and became fast friends. Chaplin invited Einstein and his wife to visit him in his home often. When Chaplin's film City Lights was released, he again invited Einstein and his wife Elsa as his special guests. They arrived together sporting identical black ties for the event.

There's still much more to know about Einstein than what is already published. Many speculate that there is still more to discover about Einstein that's still hidden under wraps. Conspiracy theories about him often surface but most have never been proven.

Chapter 7:
Einstein's Most Quotable Quotes and Other Life Lessons

The life of Einstein has become an inspiration to many. He has been quoted saying the most profound words of wisdom and has imparted many different important life lessons. Here are some of Einstein's most quotable quotes and best life lessons.

Life Lessons From Albert Eistein

1. Einstein taught people not to discriminate – Einstein was an advocate of human rights and fought for the rights of African Americans. He once made a speech at a Lincoln University in Pennsylvania. This speech was important because it was the first university that gave a college degree to black students.

   When Princeton's Nassau Inn turned away opera singer Marian Anderson because she was black, Einstein told the singer to stay at his home as his guest. Every time she came to town, she always stayed at Einstein's place and she was always welcome there. Ever since then, the two enjoyed a friendship that lasted until Einstein died in 1955.

2. Einstein taught people to believe in their abilities and not let gender, race or standing in life stop them from reaching their dreams – A little girl named Tyfanny from South Africa corresponded with Einstein constantly at the height of his career. She once wrote Einstein that she loved science and hated the fact that she was a girl. She also so said that she hoped that

Einstein didn't mind that she was a girl. Einstein wrote back to the little girl stating simply that:

I do not mind that you are a girl, but the main thing is that you yourself do not mind. There is no reason for it.

This response teaches people that being a girl, or being black, or being handicapped, or different in any way is not something to be ashamed of. He taught people that anybody regardless of race, gender and standing in life has a chance to make something out of themselves and should never let these factors hinder their success.

3. Einstein taught people about living simply, humbly and modestly – despite his fame and fortune Einstein never lived in lavishness. Even with all the accolades and the recognition that he garnered, he remained humble and never boastful.

4. Einstein taught people to feed their imagination and share it with others – Einstein's imagination helped to develop theories, and also experiments that would prove these theories as well. He had always been a dreamy child according to his sister and his imagination paved the way for some of the most ground breaking theories to ever be discovered and proven. He was once even quoted saying *"Imagination is more important than knowledge. For knowledge is limited to all we now know and understand, while imagination embraces the entire world, and all there ever will be to know and understand."*

5. Einstein taught people not to be afraid to make mistakes – Einstein's most famous equation didn't just

come to him in a dream. He formulated it and perfected it over time using a series of experiments. Along the way, he made several mistakes and encountered a lot of roadblocks. But his mistakes never deterred him from pursuing the answers to his questions. He knew that mistakes are a part of life and that they impart invaluable lessons that you will never get when you always succeed.

Quotes From The Genius

Throughout his lifetime Einstein was a walking jumble of important life quotes. Some of his most famous ones are listed below:

1. *Two things are infinite: the universe and human stupidity. And I'm not sure about the former.* – Einstein did not generally think that man is stupid or anything but he did say in this quote that there are so many stupid things that people do for some reason or another.

2. *Insanity: doing the same thing over and over again and expecting different results.* - This is one of Einstein's most quotable quotes.

3. *Peace cannot be kept by force; it can only be achieved by understanding.* – His call for nuclear disarmament and an end to the wars made him utter these words. He condemned the use of weapons that threaten to destroy humanity and hated the thought that he once became instrumental to the destruction of thousands of innocent lives. Even now, this quote holds true regarding the discord between different religions of the

world and misunderstanding from different world leaders. Until understanding is achieved, there may never be peace on earth.

4. *When you are courting a nice girl an hour seems like a second. When you sit on a red-hot cinder a second seems like an hour. That's relativity.* – Einstein was once asked to explain the theory of relativity in layman's terms and this was his answer.

5. *A happy man is too satisfied with the present to dwell on the future* - in this quote, Einstein is telling you that in order to be happy you must live in the present, forget the past and not worry about the future. Everything will fall into place eventually and you will find that everything happens for a reason.

6. *The difference between stupidity and genius is that genius has limits* – Einstein was probably often stumped by how much stupidity man possesses that he was often quoted with some quip about it.

7. *It's not that I'm so smart it's just that I stay with problems longer* - this quote urges people to keep on persevering. Einstein never gave up on his dreams even when nobody thought they were worth anything. He was lucky enough to have a family that supported him even when he wanted to renounce his citizenship just to avoid military service.

8. *Life is like riding a bicycle. To keep your balance, you must keep moving* – Einstein urged people not to keep moving forward.

9. *The measure of intelligence is the ability to change –* Einstein knew that change is inevitable. Knowing this, he urged people to try to adapt to the changes that are happening to the world.

10. *Only those who attempt the absurd can achieve the impossible.* – Einstein did not become great because he did something that already had been done. He always strived to find the answers to some of physics' most difficult questions and usually succeeded. He urged people to go with their gut and try anything that seemed absurd and unusual. You'll never know if your absurd idea could become the next best thing.

These are just some of Einstein's most memorable life lessons and quotes. Most of them have been turned into memes and posters and have been circulating the net for a long time. It seems that Einstein was never at a loss for life lessons on any kind of topic available.

Albert Einstein lived a full, exciting and eventful life. He achieved a lot for himself and for science. He gave his life to advance man's knowledge of the world. Even in his death, as in the case of his brain being studied by various scientists hoping to unlock the secrets to his genius, he was still providing knowledge to mankind. His life and works continue to be an inspiration to everyone whose lives he has touched. Until now, his theories and works can be felt through modern technology. His quotable quotes and life lessons still hold true even under modern circumstances. Though he is long gone, he won't be forgotten for centuries to come.

Conclusion

Thanks again for taking the time to read this book!

I hope that you learned a lot about Albert Einstein and picked up more than a handful of lessons from his life journey. You do not have to be a genius to live a fulfilled life. You only need to dare to push yourself to go beyond your limitations and reach for your dreams. Just like Einstein did, do not waver in what you truly believe in, no matter if the odds are not in your favor. Perseverance and determination will bring you success. Of course, don't forget to enjoy your personal life all throughout your journey.

If you enjoyed this book, please take the time to leave me a review on Amazon. I appreciate your honest feedback, and it really helps me to continue producing high quality books.